In the Valley of Bottled Poetry

Napa Valley's Architectural Survivors

by

Denzil Verardo, Ph.D.

and

Jennie Dennis Verardo

THE BOXWOOD PRESS

Pacific Grove, California

Distributed by
The Boxwood Press
183 Ocean View Blvd.
Pacific Grove, CA 93950
(408) 375-9110

ISBN:0-910286-53-1

Printed in U.S.A.

Foreword

WHEN JACK AND ELAINE Hesemeyer first approached us with the idea of a book based on Otto Hesemeyer's "Survivors of the Past" pen and ink drawings, we little realized the feelings and reminiscences that those "Survivors" evoked in so many Napa Valley "pioneers." The textual portions of this work were greatly enhanced by the memories and anecdotes so readily and willingly provided by several of these long-time residents.

We have attempted to provide a history of the Napa Valley for those interested in a detailed background, while at the same time allowing for each pen and ink drawing to stand on its own for those who want a minimum of detailed information on each print. Thus a detailed history of the Napa Valley precedes the actual drawings and their accompanying stories.

Our warm gratitude goes to W.W. "Jack" Lyman, Lelia "Lee" Crouch, John Wichels, Jeff Hesemeyer, the Napa County Historical Society, Yolande Beard, Mrs. Mark Bauer, Bill Grummer, as well as all of the others who aided in making this work both accurate and interesting; and, of course to Jack and Elaine, without whose faith and support this work would not have even been possible.

Denzil and Jennie Verardo
June 1983

Otto Hesemeyer
(1888-1977)

About The Artist

Otto Hesemeyer was born on April 25, 1888 in San Francisco, the son of an immigrant German pharmacist and his wife. Early awareness of his natural ability in art led to Hesemeyer's acceptance by, and attendance at, the California School of Arts and Crafts and the Mark Hopkins Art Institute. In 1912 he married, and 50 years later he and Florence were to celebrate their Golden Anniversary in the same spot that they had spent their honeymoon—the Napa Valley. In 1916, Otto Hesemeyer began working for the Schmidt Lithograph Company in San Francisco, where he soon excelled in the field of commercial art. In this era virtually all art work for commercial use was done by hand painting or drawing methods, rather than by photography. While working in the Bay Area, Otto received several commercial art awards including the coveted Pacific Coast Advertising Association trophy for the best display of original commercial art.

After "retiring" in 1962, the Hesemeyers moved to Napa Valley. Otto soon became known as one of the Valley's outstanding artists. Not only did he continue to do commercial art, but he also painted a 6 x 10 foot oil mural for the Christian Brothers at Mont LaSalle for the Liturgical Conference at the Seattle World's Fair. He designed the emblem used by the City of St. Helena on its vehicles after having his design selected by the St. Helena Chamber of Commerce in the city-wide competition. Otto was awarded life membership in the Upper Napa Valley Associates in 1963 for his "generous contributions" which included their stationery design and mailing pieces. He also completed a series of pen and ink drawings entitled "Survivors of the Past" which were to have been part of a local history book. Unfortunately, he died in October 1977, at the age of 89, before these drawings could be published. His art remains, and reminds us that he was one of the Napa Valley's truly fine artists.

Contents

A Look Back   1

IN MANY WAYS, the history of the Napa Valley reflects the history of California. Although the Valley is not large or strategically located commercially or militarily, much of the drama of early and modern California has been played out in and around it.

For thousands of years, the only human inhabitants of the Napa Valley were the native Wappo Indians. During the 16th, 17th and 18th centuries, while Europeans were exploring and settling the east and west coasts of North America, the Napa Valley lay undiscovered and unexplored by white men.

During the latter part of the 18th century and the early part of the 19th, the Spanish explorers and missionaries were busy establishing missions, pueblos and presidios along the California coast. Beginning in 1769 at San Diego, they attempted to claim and settle their new territory by building missions to Christianize and civilize the local natives. By 1817, the Spanish had pushed the chain of missions and *assistencias* up the coast to San Rafael. In 1812, Russian trappers and fur traders had established an outpost on the northern California coast at Fort Ross. It wasn't until 1823 however, two years after Mexico had won its independence from Spain, that the now self-reliant Mexicans acknowledged that the Russians might prove a threat to them.

Determined to stop Russian intrusion into what it considered its territory, the Mexican government sent out the soldiers Francisco Castro and Jose Sanchez and Father Jose Altimura as the heads of a party to find a suitable site for a mission north of San Francisco Bay. They explored the area from Petaluma to Sonoma, Napa and Suisun and in 1823, the decision was made to establish the mission at Sonoma. During the 1820's, the Napa Valley was used for raising cattle, sheep and horses for the support of the Sonoma Mission.

A few new but crude methods of cultivation were introduced during this period, but for the most part, the Spanish period created few changes in the landscape. The Spanish did, however, manage to nearly decimate the native Indian population throughout California, principally by bringing with them diseases against which the natives had no immunity. In the case of the Napa Valley, it was smallpox. '

In 1827, a young adventurer, Guy Fling, became the first American to visit the Napa Valley. Four years later, Fling led another American, George Yount, into this valley. Yount was completely taken by the beauty of the Napa Valley and reportedly declared, "In such a place I would like to clear the land and make my home; in such a place I would like to live and die."

Later, while Yount was in Sonoma doing repair work on some mission buildings, he became aquainted with General Mariano Vallejo. Vallejo was impressed with Yount's ability and energy; and as a reward for his work on the mission and Vallejo's new home in Sonoma, he desired to give Yount something more. Vallejo learned of Yount's desire to settle permanently in the area, and offered to help him secure a land grant. After Yount became a naturalized Mexican citizen and had converted to Catholicism, the two prerequisites for land ownership, the General's cousin, Governor Juan Alvarado helped facilitate the grant. In March, 1836, two square leagues of land (approximately 11,814 acres) were granted to Jorge Concepcion (George) Yount. This was the first tract of land granted by the Mexican government in the Napa Valley. It extended from present-day Yountville to just north of Rutherford.

During this period, virtually all of the Americans who came west were in search of wealth. Most were trappers or traders and many blazed trails that later settlers would follow. And, although the Napa Valley may have offered pelts, Kit Carson was the only mountain man to visit the Napa Valley before the 1840s.

In 1837, an Englishman who later had a great impact on the Napa Valley, Dr. Edward Turner Bale, landed in Monterey. At this time, Monterey was one of the larger settlements in California, a presidio and the port of entry for most vessels. California, in 1837, was a sparsely-populated wilderness. George Yount and a Dr. John Marsh who had settled near Mt. Diablo were two of the very few Americans in the interior. It would be three more years before Sutter would attempt to civilize the inland valleys with his settlement on the Sacramento River. Bale was employed by Mariano Vallejo as Surgeon-in-Chief for the Mexican Army. As such, he travelled between San Francisco (then called Yerba Buena) and Monterey ministering to the soldiers' needs. He soon built a reputation not only as a man of medicine, but also as one with a penchant for alcohol. He ran up bills for many pesos' worth of liquor at a time, and soon became a famous, and infamous, figure on the early California scene.

Bale's temperament was erratic and he was often quarrelsome. Nevertheless, in 1839, Bale had married Maria Ignacia Soberanes, a niece of General Mariano Vallejo and Salvador Vallejo. In 1841 he became full citizen of Mexican California. Through the influence of the Vallejo family, Bale obtained a grant of four square leagues of land in the Upper Napa Valley. The grant, renamed by Bale *Rancho Carne Humana* (Human Flesh Ranch) a play upon the local Indian's tribal name *Callojomanas,* comprised the Napa Valley north from Yount's Caymus grant. As surveyed for the United States patent ultimately confirming title, it contained 17,962 acres.

Although the Vallejo family had helped secure Bale's position and land, his relationship with his inlaws was not always amicable. Ill feeling between Salvador Vallejo and Bale came to a head in June, 1844. By virtue of his military rank as captain, Vallejo had Bale publicly flogged in Sonoma on the grounds that Bale was circulating rumors that cast doubt on Salvador Vallejo's veracity. Following this indignity, Dr. Bale left Sonoma for a time, but he returned accompanied by 14 other men. Bale found Vallejo and shot him twice from behind, grazing Vallejo's neck and hitting Vallejo's companion, Cayetano Juarez in the jawbone. Bale, put under arrest by General Mariano Vallejo's police, was tried and found guilty. But Bale was soon released by Governor Micheltorena. It had been suggested that the Governor feared otherwise to have trouble with the English consul.

MEANWHILE Russian influence was again being felt in Northern California. In 1841, a party said to have included Princess Helena de Gargarina, niece of the Czar, explored the mountains northeast of Calistoga, leaving a plaque on the mountain top, and, according to one account. naming the peak of Mt. St. Helena in honor of Helena, the Empress of Russia.

A few years later, in 1845, Bale began selling off pieces of his grant in order to raise the capital to make improvements to secure his ownership. A great influx of Americans was beginning in the Valley. Trappers returning east and entrepreneurs envisioning the wealth they could acquire, encouraged Americans to emigrate west with their tales of abundance, good land, and agreeable weather on the western side of the Sierra Nevada.

In 1841, a group known as the Bidwell-Bartleson party had left Independence, Missouri for California. In this group was a man who was later to head his own parties out and then to have an impact on the development of this area—Joseph Chiles. The real significance of the Bidwell-Bartleson expedition though was that in its success, it was an entering wedge for wholesale immigration to the Pacific Coast, and it marked the beginning of a steady current of migration to California.

The best known of these immigrant parties was the Donner Party, perhaps because it was one of the less fortunate, and most-publicized as a result. Here too there is a tie with the Napa Valley. In the party as it left Missouri were Reason P. Tucker and his family. At Fort Hall, they were warned by experienced guides that they were starting out too late that year, and might easily be caught by early snows in the Sierras. They stubbornly insisted on going ahead, although the Tuckers disagreed with the Donners over which route to take, so they split up. Tucker with his six wagons, his wife and several sons took the older route. The Donners tried the new route that Lansford Hastings had advertised. The Tuckers crossed the Sierra Nevada at Yuba Pass and arrived at Bear River in California in the fall of 1846. A month later, they moved on to Sutter's Fort to stay for the winter. In January, 1847, a few of the survivors of the Donner Party arrived at Bear River to get help for the other members who had survived that tragic winter. Messengers were sent to Sutter's Fort for men and supplies and Tucker was appointed captain of one of the rescue parties. Tucker's group was the first to reach the survivors of the Donner tragedy, who were then taken to Sutter's Fort. Tucker personally took over responsibility for caring for one of the survivors, Sarah Graves Fosdick, who had lost both her husband and her parents in that ordeal. When the Tucker family arrived in the Napa Valley, Mrs. Fosdick was with them. Tucker and his son each bought tracts of land just south of what is now Calistoga. And the Tucker family soon became influential members of the valley community. Mrs. Fosdick was the teacher of the first school in Napa County, opened up soon after her arrival just opposite Bale's Grist Mill. It should be noted that these American settlers and their families were not seeking gold or riches in coming to California, but rather a better way of life. They were willing to suffer untold hardship to achieve it.

By some accounts, both Bale and Yount, encouraged Americans to settle in the Napa Valley, feeling more secure as the number of their English-speaking countrymen increased. By other accounts, Bale and Yount encountered difficulties with American squatters, and tried to keep them off their lands. With or without the approval of Dr. Bale or Señor Yount, the western migration was adding considerably to the white population of the Napa Valley. By the middle of the 1800s, much of the valley was in the process of cultivation, thus marking the beginning of the end of the pastoral period in Napa County history.

AMERICANS, as seems their nature, were beginning to exploit the natural resources. Having contracted with Ralph Kilburn to build and operate his sawmill, Dr. Bale began to have timber cut on his land. John York, who built the first permanent cabin in Calistoga (or Hot Springs, as it was then known), brought the logs down to Bale's Mill. In 1846, Bale having sold off more land, began work on his grist mill. Being perpetually cash-short, he offered Florentine

Kellogg 600 acres of his land for doing the iron work for his mill. Dr. Bale seems to have generous to a fault. When James Clyman had passed through the Napa Valley in 1845, he made a vivid note of its dry desolation and lack of cultivation. With the construction of Bale's grist mill and several others in the valley and the influx of farmers from the east, the means were becoming available to make grain cultivation more profitable and the valley less desolate.

The new immigrants, like the Tuckers and the Yorks and Kilburns were a different sort than the earlier settlers like Bale and Yount. The newcomers were farmers for the most part rather than businessmen or ranchers in the Spanish style. They did not intermarry, but brought their families and their possessions with them. They formed their own isolated communities inland, apart from the Spanish and Mexican settlements. They rarely associated with the Californios, for whom they had a certain contempt. Most felt that the Californios had undeserved wealth in the extensive land grants. Likewise, the Californios didn't find the Americans especially attractive. Under these circumstances, friction could not be avoided indefinitely.

The United States Government was at this time, also interested in California. It was afraid that the inadequate Mexican control of Alta California might encourage British seizure of the province. The British were already a threat in the Oregon Territory, jointly occupied by the United States and England. The Russians were also moving south from Alaska, and Fort Ross posed a definite threat in American eyes. In 1823, President Monroe expressed the idea, later incorporated in the Monroe Doctrine, that the United States would not permit the extension of European powers in the Americas. California was a strategic location guarding the Pacific, and the United States did not look favorably either upon British or Russian control of the territory. After bungling an attempt to buy Northern California for half-a-million dollars in 1835, the U.S. Government sent out "scientific expeditions" to investigate the Pacific Coast.

In 1843, John Fremont was sent on two expeditions west. In 1844, President Polk appointed Thomas Larkin, U.S. Consul to California, as a confidential agent under instructions from the U.S. Department of State. He kept the U.S. Government informed on the feelings of native Californians. He was to encourage American immigration to California and assure Californians that, if they should separate from Mexico, the United States would receive them if they so wished. Larkin's task was to win Californians over the idea of separation from Mexico and to build up the desirability of their becoming part of the United States.

Fremont made a third expedition to California in the spring of 1846. There were 62 well-armed soldiers in his band. Alarmed by rumors that the Mexican government was about to forbid further American immigration into California, and the news that Californians were inciting Indians to attack American settlers, the Americans began gathering at Fremont's camp near Sutter's settlement for protection.

It was decided to intercept a group of Mexicans who were moving some horses from Sonoma to Governor Castro's camp near Santa Clara. Led by Ezekiel Merritt, the action was designed to start a revolt. However, the Mexicans thought it was theft rather than rebellion. On June 12, 1846, another group started out from Fremont's camp in the Sacramento Valley and came through the Napa Valley on their way to Sonoma. Several locals joined the group which had stopped at Dr. Bale's Grist Mill. These included: Samuel Kelsey, John Grigsby, David Hudson, William Hargrove, Harrison Pierce, Nathan Coombs and Elias Barrett. They then proceeded to capture Sonoma in order to get possession of all the territory north of San Francisco and declare independence. They "took" General Mariano Vallejo and a Lieutenant Colonel and a Captain, who were all captured in their sleep, and who were good enough to supply the brandy and help word a formal statement of terms whose end product was the California Republic.

A lone star and a grizzly bear on a field of white, bordered underneath by a red stripe, all crudely painted by one of the men, became the flag of the new Republic. The Bear Flag Republic had no constitution, no officials, no law. It did cause hostilities in the Napa Valley, since not everyone supported the revolt. Feuding between neighbors was common, and the period was charged with emotionalism and high tension. Once the outbreak had taken place, Fremont and his men returned to join the movement, and a militia was organized to patrol north of San Francisco Bay. The militia fought only one battle, the Battle of Olompali, in the vicinity of Petaluma. One Californian and two horses were the casualities, and neither side could claim a victory.

When the Bear Flag Republic was less than two months old, war broke out between the United States and Mexico over the annexation of Texas to the U.S. California was occupied by American forces, and the change of government took place without bloodshed. The Bear Flag Republic had been in existence less than 60 days, extended over no more than 40 miles of territory, but it made a lasting contribution to California in giving us our state flag.

Two years after California's "independence," on January 24, 1848, James Marshall was to make a discovery that would have an incredible impact on all of California. In the tailrace of Sutter's new saw-mill at Coloma near Sacramento, Marshall found gold! And it was Sam Brannan in his San Francisco newspaper who announced it to the world! The rush was on to California and the gold fields. While many settlements were depleted of residents by the pros-pect of quick wealth, most of the Napa Valley's residents either remained on their farms or returned after a quick trip to the Mother Lode. E.T. Bale was an exception. While his mill was continuing to grind the golden grain of Napa Valley into flour, and thus provide a living for many families, Bale set out to make his fortune in the gold fields. He did not strike it rich, but did contract a fever from which he never recovered. Realizing that he was dying, Bale sold off much of his property to insure his widow would not be left with his debt.

Down valley from Dr. Bale, Mr. J.H. Still had erected a building and established a general mer-chandise store in 1853, in what was to become St. Helena. In 1855, Mr. Still announced that he would donate lots to any persons who would erect business houses on the same. Mr. Still is also credited with naming the town "from the name given to the Div-ision of the Sons of Temperance once established there about that time...On account of the fine view obtained of St. Helena Mountain, the Division was named St. Helena, and the Division gave the name

to the town." (County History, 1873). Thus began the town of St. Helena, which was officially incorpo-rated in 1876. The Napa Valley was indeed becoming more civilized and much less desolate. In fact, Napa County was second only to Santa Clara county as California's leading wheat producer in the 1850's.

In the late 1850's, another event occurred which was to drastically change the face of the Napa Val-ley. Caroline Bale, daughter of E.T. Bale married Charles Krug, and upon the land left to her, they planted grapes. Krug's enterprise prospered. He was an expert winemaker and was continually alert to new methods to improve the quality of his wine. The Krugs' ranch and vineyard was one of the most productive in the whole Napa Valley and their hos-pitality was known far and wide. His wines were to gain international reputation.

In 1859, another man touched the Napa Valley, and it would never be the same after his arrival. Sam Brannan, California's first millionaire, the man who organized the Committee of Vigilance in San Fran-cisco, and who announced the gold rush after first buying up mercantile establishments in both San Francisco and Sutterville, was a man of many sides and may forever puzzle historians as to his real motives. While Samuel Brannan may not have "founded" Calistoga, and there remains some doubt about his naming of the resort town, no one can discount the impact that this man had on the Napa Valley and California.

During the 1860's, while most of the rest of the country was involved with the beginning of the Civil War, the upper Napa Valley's star was rising. Brannan was developing the town of Calistoga and J.H. Still's St. Helena was progressing nicely. With the promise of a railroad connecting with Napa, and thence the rest of the state, the times boded well. In the 1860's, silver and quicksilver were discovered in the Mayacamas Mountains northeast of Calistoga. Peak production was during 1874-78 when mines such as the famous Silverado, Excelsior, Oat Hill and the Helen were large enough to have settlements grow up around them. The silver soon played out and after World War I, the price of mercury or quicksilver fell, so the mines were all abandoned. The flavor of those earlier mining endeavors and the romanticism of the "Silverado" era were perhaps expressed best by Robert Louis Stevenson in his *Silverado Squatters*.

The Napa Valley had changed much by the time that Stevenson was chronicling its characters. It is interesting to compare the Napa Valley Stevenson described with James Clyman's impressions left after a trip through the valley in 1845. First Stevenson:

"...soon we were away from all signs of the sea's neighbor, mounting an inland, irrigated valley. A great variety of oaks stood, now severally, now in a becoming grove, among the fields and vineyards. The towns were compact, in about equal proportions, of bright new wooden houses and great and growing forest trees; and the chapel bell on the engine sounded most festally that sunny Sunday, as we drew up at one green town after another, with townsfolk trooping in their Sunday's best to see the strangers, with sun sparkling on the clean houses, and great domes of foliage humming overhead in the breeze." (*Siverado Squatters,* Robert Louis Stevenson, 1880)

Then Clyman: (Note that grammatical and spelling errors are original author's)

"Left Mr. Younts...Took a northern direction up the vally of the creek on which Mr. Younts mills are situated...
"5 or 6 miles above passed the farm house of Dr. Bales this hous looked desolate Enough standing on a dry plane near a dry Black volcanic mountain allmost destitute of vegitation no fields garden or any kind of cultivation to been seen and about 10 or 12 Indians lying naked in

the scorching sun finished the scenery of this rural domain."

In 1863-65, a great drought struck the valley. It, more than anything helped accomplish the break-up of the old ranchos. Ranchers had to sell great portions of their herds because there was no feed, and this in a valley whose main agricultural product had been grain.

By the early 1870's, the Napa Valley and most of California were Americanized. Overnight millionaires were no longer materializing, due to the end of the gold and silver rushes, and most of Napa Valley had settled down to work for a living.

Viticulture had become an important industry in the valley. Men like Jacob Schram, Gestave Neibaum, the Beringer Brothers, and, of course, Charles Krug were beginning to know a prosperity born of the vine. In California in the 1870's the grape and wine "industry" employed more labor than any other branch of farming and indeed was encouraged by the State because of the relative ease of production and high prices associated with winemaking. The prosperity of the late 1860's and early 1870's had all of the earmarks of a boom. However, in September 1873, America fell into one of the worst depressions it had known. The California wine industry was not seriously affected until 1876, when besides the general economic situation, winemakers had to deal with both an overproduction of wine and a generally poor quality product. With steady improvement in the wine produced, the industry was able to stage a revival after 1878. In addition to improvement in quality, the California wine industry also benefitted tremendously from the phylloxera epidemic that caused the failure of many French vineyardists and the destruction of thousands of acres of vines in France, assuring new markets for the California wine and diminishing competition. Good times had finally arrived for many struggling Napa Valley vintners.

At the end of the 19th century tragedy struck the Napa Valley and California's other wine-producing regions. The deadly plant louse, phylloxera, appeared and not only destroyed thousands of acres of vineyards, but threatened the very foundations of the industry. Men like Charles Krug were destroyed financially. By 1893, half of the vineyards in Napa County were seriously infected and others were at least mildly diseased. During this depressed period, grapes could be bought for $10 a ton and wine was 25¢ a gallon. Many of the small growers just gave up and moved away.

California's vineyards managed to recover rather

rapidly from the phylloxera devastation though, using louse-resistant American rootstock to replace their ravaged vineyards. By 1895, the California wine industry had reestablished itself. Until the passage of the 18th amendment with its "prohibition" of production or use of alcoholic beverages, the vineyardists of California produced better grapes and superior wines than at any time in the past.

Between the turn of the century and 1915, when local prohibition movements started gaining momentum, the wine industry experienced an increase in both acreage and wine production. Profits and consumption during this period seem to have varied both with changes in the business cycle and the actual price of the wine. Wine was still a luxury for most and was far from being a national beverage.

While prohibition did curtail the production of wine, except for "sacramental" or "medicinal" purposes, at the same time there was a marked increase in wine-grape shipments, especially to the east coast. With uncooled box cars and slow transit, some wine grapes arrived in the east as an almost-finished product. With the repeal of Prohibition and ever-improving quality in the wine produced, it became increasingly profitable to have vineyards.

Despite the potential for success in the wine indus-try, it wasn't until late in this century that the Napa Valley became such a homogenous agriculture region, relying so heavily on the vine. As late as 1947, descriptions of the valley show the diversity that existed here:

"The journey beyond Rutherford, toward Mount St. Helena looming ahead, is through groves of olives and figs and walnuts, orchards of apricot, cherry, prune, plum, pear and peach trees. This countryside is one great landscape garden. At St. Helena, you are in the valley of the vine..." (*California: An Intimate View,* Aubrey Drury, 1947)

Wine is now a leading commercial product of the Napa Valley, and its reputation for quality is respected throughout the world. Tourists are again discovering the special charm of the area and its unique hot-springs-borne, health-giving waters, and pleasure-assuring wine. One can easily see how beautiful and successful this very special valley has become. Now we will give you a glimpse of how it achieved this success by looking at some of its "survivors of the past."

The Old Bale Mill, 1846   2

WHEN EDWARD TURNER BALE arrived in Monterey, Alta California in 1837, it was as an English doctor shipwrecked with little but his skill as a physician, and a seemingly innate sense of audacity. By the time he died twelve years later, he had become a Mexican citizen with an aristocratic wife, three daughters and two sons, and owner of most of the upper Napa Valley and of several profitable businesses therein. Bale's skill as a physician and surgeon, and his reputation for drinking and erratic behavior may well be forgotten eventually; but he unknowingly left a monument in this valley by which he will long be remembered—his grist mill.

Through family connections, Dr. Bale had been granted an almost 18,000 acre tract of land in the Napa Valley in 1841. Using profit-sharing and small parcels of land as payment in lieu of cash, Bale had built a sawmill, his adobe and by 1846, was prepared to begin construction of a grist mill. Bale had planted some of his acreage in wheat and he could see the opportunity to profit from milling his own grain and that of his neighbors in a more modern grist mill rather than by the older, less-profitable methods of handmilling.

When the grist mill was completed, it had a 20-foot overshot wheel (overshot signifies that water entered from the top of the wheel). However, this wheel apparently did not provide enough power during dry summers and was replaced, in the early 1850's, by the larger 36-foot wheel which can be seen today. This is the largest overshot wheel west of the Mississippi and may be the largest still in operating condition in the United States. The wheel itself weighs about $5\frac{1}{2}$ tons and turned at five or six revolutions per minute, generating approximately 40 horsepower. Water for the wheel was diverted from Mill Creek into a mill pond formed by a dam. A ditch and wooden flume system then conveyed the water from the millpond to the top of the waterwheel. Having completed its task of turning the wheel, the water flowed back across what is now Highway 29 into Mill Creek. The grinding stones for the mill were initially of local stone, but were later replaced by French stones of a superior quality. Originally wooden cogs operated the mill, but they were later replaced by iron gears. According to a first-hand account by George Tucker, an early settler in the valley, the wooden cogs made a considerable racket when the mill was operating.

The mill must have been a center of attention in the upper Napa Valley, not only because of its spectacular size and the amount of noise it generated, but because wheat production was on the increase,

The Old Bale Mill, 1846, Napa Valley, California

The Bale Grist Mill today. The wooden waterwheel was the largest west of the Mississippi. The Mill, recently reconstructed, is open to the public as a unit of the State Park System.

becoming the valley's major crop. The status of miller was a well-respected one, and the millers at the Bale Grist Mill appear to have been people of some stature in the community. The granary building adjoining the mill being a large vacant space, was used for meetings, dances and other social events as late as the 1870's. Originally there had been a raised platform with steps on both sides connecting the two buildings.

In 1879, the great wheel was to turn for the last time. The mill had passed to Bale's heirs upon his dealth in 1849 and it remained in their hands until 1860, when it was sold to Ralph Ellis and Edward Irwin. Ellis installed a steam engine during the drought of 1862-64 to aid in powering the millstones. The mill again changed hands in 1868. And, in 1871, the Reverend Theodore Lyman purchased the mill and the surrounding acreage, as much to protect the water rights of the property he had acquired on the other side of the creek as to own the mill. By 1879, wheat acreage and production had declined to the point that custom milling was uneconomical, and the rise of more efficient milling operations made the use of the waterwheel impractical. In the 1880's, the Lymans installed a water turbine to power the mill's operation, but the mill remained a small custom milling operation and did not compete with the newer, larger mills in the county. The last commercial use of the grindstones was in 1905.

In 1923, Mr. W.W. Lyman, Sr. died and the property passed to his widow who deeded the mill to the Native Sons of the Golden West, Napa Parlor, for preservation as a public monument. In 1941, Napa County became the owner of the mill, and continued the efforts at preservation begun by the Native Sons. In 1974, the mill was turned over to the State of California and became Bale Grist Mill State Historic Park and a registered National Historic Landmark. Restoration work was begun on the mill by the California Department of Parks & Recreation in 1980, and through public bond money and generous donations, the mill will again be grinding grain.

Original Charles Krug Family Stables, 1888 Present Charles Krug Winery Aging Cellars

3

IN 1860, eleven years after Dr. E.T. Bale's death, his daughter Caroline married Charles Krug. Part of her dowry was some 540 acres of Napa Valley land upon which they planted vineyards. Krug was not a novice to winemaking when he began this venture, though. At the age of 22, he had come to America from Prussia. He taught at the Free Thinkers' School in Philadelpia until 1848 when political unrest in Prussia caused him to return to aid an attempt to overthrow the reactionary parliament. The revolt failed, and Krug was imprisoned. He escaped in 1849 and made his way back to Philadelphia, where he became an American citizen.

Three years later, in 1852, Krug came to California. He tried his hand at farming in San Mateo, but soon gave that up and found work first in a private gold establishment, and then as clerk of the refining department of the U.S. Mint in San Francisco.

He saved carefully and in 1858, was able to purchase 20 acres of property in Sonoma which he planted a vineyard. Coincidentally or not, Count Agostin Haraszthy, who is known as the father of California viticulture, was also employed at the San Francisco Mint about this time and also established

his vineyards in the Sonoma Valley. Both men had previously been engaged in agriculture in San Mateo, it would seem a reasonable certainty that they knew each other. In fact, both were related by marriage to General Mariano Vallejo—Krug by his marriage to Vallejo's grandniece and Haraszthy by his son's marriage to Vallejo's daughter. Just how well they knew each other and how much guidance or counsel on viticulture may have been exchanged is not known for certain. While Haraszthy was innovating in the Sonoma Valley, Krug was working in the Napa Valley. In 1858, Krug made some 1200 gallons of wine for John Pachett of Napa using a small cider press. It was the first wine made in Napa County by other than the old Spanish process. This accomplishment established Krug as a pioneer winemaker in the valley, and his services became in great demand. In 1860, he moved to St. Helena and later that year married Caroline Bale.

The Krugs' ranch and vineyard was one of the most productive in the Napa Valley. Krug himself was an expert winemaker and was constantly experimenting with new methods to improve the quality of his wine. His reputation for creating fine wines

Original Charles Krug family, stables, 1888. Present Charles Krug Winery ageing cellers, Napa Valley, California.

This "stable" was considered the best of its kind in the Napa Valley in 1880. Its architecture still reflects the social prestige which was typified by one's horses and carriages. Today it is part of the Krug's aging cellars.

grew and was matched by his family's reputation for their hospitality, and the grand parties that they gave. Mr. W.W. Lyman, who was born in the Napa Valley 98 years ago and raised in the house next to Bale's Mill remembers Charles Krug as a man "of medium height and slender build and quick and active in his movements. He talked a great deal in a resonant voice. As I remember him, his hair and beard were grizzled. He had a full head of hair, and he wore his beard short—a Scotch Terrier sort of beard...Mrs. Krug was a large woman with well-cut features and a dark complexion showing her Spanish blood. I remember especially her voice was clear and pleasant."

The entire Krug family seems to have been well-respected in the valley. Mr. Krug was active in local affairs, serving as the first president of the St. Helena Viticulture Association as well as being a California State Viticulture Commission member.

For a family of such prominence, it would only be fitting that their estate reflect their success and good taste. Indeed, that was the goal when Krugs had their stable and wine cellar built. And, since social prestige then depended a great deal upon the horses and carriages one owned; and since wine had given the family its status, it was very logical to erect those two buildings before the main house. Both buildings were large and of excellent architecture and were the best of their kind in the Napa Valley in the 1880's. In contrast, the Krug house was small, resembling an enlarged cottage. Unfortunately, before a fitting house could be built, a depression and the phylloxera epidemic hit the valley and Krug was devastated financially.

Charles Krug died in 1892, with his fortunes like those of other vintners at a low ebb. The winery continued to decline until 1943, when Cesare Mondavi and sons purchased it from James K. Moffitt. Mondavi, proprietor of the Sunny St. Helena Winery and holdings in Lodi "bought the place for his sons, Peter, now (1943) in the Army and Robert, manager of Sunny St. Helena Winery," according to a St. Helena newspaper account.

The stables are now a part of the Charles Krug Winery and are a State Historic Landmark. It is exciting to imagine though what the Krugs' home might have been like after viewing the elegance of their stable.

Sam Brannan Home, 1860 4

IN THE SAME YEAR that Charles Krug was establishing himself as a premier winemaker in the Napa Valley, Samuel Brannan was realizing his dream of a "Saratoga of California" in Calistoga. Sam Brannan was probably the most colorful, exciting and least-understood character to touch the valley during this, or any period. He had come to California in 1846 as the leader of East Coast Mormons fleeing persecution and seeking the Promised Land or Zion. Whether Brannan was indeed a devout Mormon who honestly felt that he had found their Zion and broke with the Church when Brigham Young refused to move west of Salt Lake City; or whether he was a scoundrel at heart who used the tithes he collected for his own betterment with no concern for the Church remains to be proven. It is known that he led the Mormon group out from New York through a difficult passage around South America and on up to Yerba Buena (San Francisco) via the Sandwich Islands (Hawaii). He did collect tithe monies which according to some accounts he used for the future economic security of the group. He had a colony established on the Stanislaus River in anticipation of the arrival of Brigham Young and the rest of the Saints. And, Brannan did travel on foot from San Francisco to Utah to tell Young of his discovery of the Promised Land. After Brannan's trip east, his attitude seems to have changed. Perhaps he did feel that he was the rightful heir to Joseph Smith's position, and Young's rebuke of his west coast Zion may have caused a final split between Brannan and his Church. Or perhaps, as some biographers claim, he was using the Mormon Church as a base and financial backer for his schemes and Young's decision to remain in Utah freed Brannan of close scrutiny. Be that as it may, it is known that Brannan returned to San Francisco, established himself as a power in the community and began to make his fortune.

He had previously established a newspaper, the second in California; and now he began to acquire land, business houses and political power. His business interests were extended up the Sacramento River to Sutterville (Sacramento) and with the gold rush adding dramatically to his mercantile business in both locations, Sam Brannan became California's first millionaire. In 1856, he was called the richest and best-known citizen of California. His income was estimated at between $250,000 and $500,000 a year.

Brannan was also very active in civic affairs, participating in everything from the introduction of European cultural activities to the city to the formation of the first Committee of Vigilance when rowdies got out of hand. He seemed to have a golden touch accompanied by unbounded energy.

He also had a desire to build a resort to rival the best in Europe. He visited and had been impressed by the hot springs resorts in Saratoga, New York while travelling with Joseph Smith's brother. When he learned of the natural hot springs and purported medicinal value of the waters of Aqua Caliente or "Hot Springs" in the upper Napa Valley, he saw a chance for his dream's fulfillment. In 1859, he purchased about 2,000 acres of upvalley land from an aging Captain Ritchie. This included geysers and hot springs as well as rich agricultural land and a large mound (small hill) which Brannan named Mt. Lincoln after the new President.

Costing half-a-million dollars, the resort originally consisted of a central area including the Hotel and bathhouses; an observatory and reservoir on Mt. Lincoln all surrounded by 25 cottages on two avenues. The cottage on the print was one of the twenty-five. Also adjoining the resort were 40 acres of race track and stables. At one time, Brannan had almost a thousand horses, many of blooded stock and 500 imported merino sheep. This was in addition to the hundreds of varieties of fruits and vegetables he experimented with, including an attempt to produce silk with silk moths. Brannan's distillery used 2500 tons of grapes in a season and produced some 90,000 gallons of brandy, some which graced tables in Europe.

Brannan was said to have paid a commission to physicians to send their patients to his resort. But that fact withstanding, the Hot Springs resort was visited often by the rich and influential of that day. The resort register listed names such as James Lick, Mark Hopkins, C.P. Huntington and one other who left us a written memory of his 1880 visit, Robert Louis Stevenson. Stevenson, his new bride and stepson occupied one of Brannan's cottages and he described the cottage and grounds in his *Silverado Squatters*:

"Alone, on the other side of the railway, stands the Springs Hotel, with its attendant cottages. The floor of the valley is extremely level to the very roots of the hills; only here and there a hillock, crowned with pines, rises like the barrow of some chieftain famed in war; and right against one of the hillocks is the Springs Hotel...A lawn runs about the house, and the lawn is in its turn surrounded by a system of little five-room cottages, each with a veranda and a weedy palm before the door. Some of the cottages are let to residents, and these are wreathed in flowers. The rest are occupied by ordinary visitors to the hotel; and a very pleasant way this is, by which you have a little country cottage of your own, without domestic burdens, and by the day or week. ...At one end of the hotel enclosure are the springs from which it takes its name, hot enough to scald a child seriously while I was there."

Brannan succeeded in building his resort and by some accounts naming the town in the process of christening his resort. It seems that he was inebriated and slurred the "Saratoga of California" into the "Calistoga of Sarafornia" and it stuck. Now he needed some way other than the stage line to get his guests up from Vallejo. Applying his subtle political pressure both in Napa county and in Sacramento, Brannan managed to have a railroad approved that was chartered by the state and subsidized by the people for the Vallejo to Calistoga line. The Napa Valley Railroad was completed to Calistoga in 1868, and Sam Brannan hosted an expedition of about 3,000 visitors up to his new resort to celebrate.

For a short time it seemed as if Brannan's dream of a lavish, successful resort might become a reality. However, too soon, the railroad proved unprofitable and was first leased and then sold. The resort, which had never been profitable, proved too much of a burden upon Brannan's sagging finances, which were also suffering from a divorce settlement which would prove to be his financial undoing.

In the spring of 1877, Samuel Brannan said his final farewells to his resort and to Calistoga. The Sacramento Savings Bank which held the mortgage on the resort ordered the sale of all Brannan's Calistoga holdings. Leland Stanford became the owner of the main resort and retained it until 1919, initially intending to establish his college there. The resort would never be the same again, though. Except for the main resort and a few cottages which were privately owned, the rest of the property was sold off in 25 to 200 acre parcels.

Three of the original cottages remain, although only the one on Wappo Street is still in its original place. The Sharpsteen Museum on Washington Street in Calistoga has one of the cottages, a State Historic Landmark, which has been restored. It is open to the public and along with a diorama of the Calistoga of the late 1800's in the museum proper, gives the modern visitor a taste of what Sam Brannan's Calistoga must have been like.

An old Sam Brannan Home. 1859-60. Napa Valley, California

Today the refurbished Sam Brannan Cottage, makes up a portion of Calistoga's Sharpsteen Museum. Originally, there were 25 such cottages built by Brannan, as well as a hotel and bathhouses, as part of his hot springs resort.

California Pacific Depot At Yountville Napa Valley, California, 1870

5

THE RAILROAD up the Napa Valley from Vallejo to Calistoga that Sam Brannan so enthusiastically promoted, was fraught with problems almost from its conception. When this Napa Valley Railroad was envisioned, Brannan was no stranger to railroading, having been the owner of 200 of the original shares of the Central Pacific Railroad and, at least a business acquaintance of railroad men like Stanford and Crocker and Huntington. Brannan was also not a newcomer to the positive effects of preferential treatment for politicians in securing a desired end. Combining his railroad and political experiences, it should have been rather simple matter for Brannan to get the 40-odd miles of road into operation.

In 1864, the Napa Valley railroad company had been organized, with C. Hartson as its first President. It had been chartered by the State Legislature, after some friendly persuasion, and was to be built chiefly by county subscriptions (bonds) of $10,000 per mile. The first few miles from Suscol (the main railhead and connection to Vallejo) to Napa City went well, except for the unexpectedly larger amount of money that it required. The railroad was forced to return to the State Legislature to get approval for additional support from the county.

Brannan, by some accounts, aided in the gentle convincing of Sacramento lawmakers, supplying them with certain amenities in order to enlighten them concerning the Napa Valley Railroad's new financial situation. The legislators were cooperative. However, it was another matter convincing county residents of the need for more revenue or even the need for the railroad itself. Valley farmers and Napa townspeople were opposed to the railroad because they viewed the extension of the line to Calistoga as a method of carrying all the freight through Napa and on to Suscol then to Vallejo. They desired a railhead at Napa City. The second bond issue was defeated by the county voters. Ultimately, after numerous other attempts to gain cooperation and support from county citizens, the railroad company sought and received a Supreme Court settlement forcing the county to issue bonds to complete the railroad. The roadway was completed to Oakville in 1867 and to St. Helena in February of 1868. In August, 1868, Brannan's dream of rail transportation to his resort was realized when the Napa Valley Railroad reached Calistoga.

To celebrate the completion of the line, Brannan hosted a grand excursion from San Francisco for 3000 culminating in a celebration complete with feasting at his Calistoga resort. It was now possible to board a steamer in San Francisco for the trip to Vallejo (bridges would not span the bay for decades) and there board a train for a pleasant and relaxing trip up the beautiful Napa Valley to Calistoga.

However, the railroad could not generate enough revenue to meet expenses, and Brannan had become unable to personally "bail out" the line. In 1869, it was sold to the California Pacific Railroad Company. It had been the original intention of the CPRR to extend the line from Calistoga to Healdsburg and through Sonoma County, Santa Rosa and the Russian River valley to Cloverdale. This intention was never carried out. It seems that the California Pacific Railroad Company was competition for the newly-strong Central Pacific Railroad Company, and that the California Pacific had planned on building a line of its own east to Ogden, Utah. Since the California Pacific route was more scenic than the Central Pacific's recently completed one, they did seem a threat to the Central Pacific's monopoly on rail traffic east.

In July, 1871, the California Pacific Railroad sold controlling interest to C.P. Huntington, Leland Stanford and Mark Hopkins for $1,597,000 and control of the company passed into the hands of the Central Pacific Railroad Company. The line from Vallejo to Calistoga eventually passed into the hands of Central Pacific's successor, Southern Pacific. The line was shut down north of the Charles Krug winery in 1966, and the tracks were ripped up.

Towns such as Oakville, Rutherford, Calistoga, St. Helena and Yountville in a large part "grew up" around the railroad. It was a vital link to the outside world, even if it did not prove financially profitable.

By the time depicted in the drawing, 1870, Yountville had become a successful little town, aided in part by the commerce provided by the railroad. Originally named Sebastopol and built upon George Yount's Caymus land grant, the town changed its name after Yount's death to honor the man who had founded it. Today, Yountville is still a succssful little town, a center of tourism and it marks the beginning of the valley of the vine.

California Pacific Depot at Yountville, Napa Valley, California, 1870

Now a portion of a major shop complex, the remnants of the California Pacific Railroad Depot still suggest the hustle and bustle of an earlier transportation era.

The next six prints are of wineries which were founded in the late 1800's. Most of the wineries saw an early prosperity which was marred first by the phylloxera epidemic in the 1880's and 1890's and then by the national economic downturn of the early 1900's. For most early wineries in the Napa Valley, the passage of the 18th Amendment in 1919, leading to prohibition on alcoholic beverages was an obstacle too great to overcome. Such was the case with the wineries illustrated here. None of these are still in orginal family hands and most are now part of a larger corporation. We have chosen to tell you only about how they were when pictured in the drawing. All are open to the public, although two allow visits by appointment only. And, the current owners can tell their winery's modern story much more adequately than our limited space would allow us to.

Burgess Cellars (Formerly Rossini Winery), 1875

6

IN 1875, a winery was constructed in the mountains on the eastern side of the valley at the 1,000 foot elevation. Founded by Carlo Rossini and his brother who were immigrants from Switzerland, the winery was part of the original family homestead. It was a small family operation until Prohibition shut it down. Carlo Rossini remained in the Napa Valley until his death in the 1930's and it is known that the winery was once again in operation when it was purchased by J. Leland (Lee) Stewart in the 1940's. Stewart, who founded Souverain Cellars, went to work on the vineyard and winery. He remodeled and enlarged the winery building and added others for storing and aging the wines.

The winery was sold again in 1970 and in 1972, eventually to Tom and Linda Burgess who renamed it Burgess Cellars and who set to work to make great wines.

This winery is a fine example of small, family concern, founded in the late 1800's which was unable to survive the ravages of phylloxera, depressed prices and prohibition. Many of these smaller wineries were forced to close down their buildings, cellars fell into disrepair and their vineyards went out of use. Within the last few decades, a revival of these old establishments seems to have begun. Some of the finest of the newer breed of winemaker have chosen to put their faith and outstanding vintages in the once-abandoned old wineries, and they are breathing new life into some of these surviving relics.

Burgess Cellars (Former Rossini Winery), *1875*

While retaining the original lines of Carlo Rossini's early winery, the photo depicts several structural changes, including window removal, to the 1875 building. It is today occupied by Burgess Cellars.

Jacob Schram's Winery, 1880

7

"About five miles northwest of St. Helena, on the eastern slope of the mountains west of the valley, is a small vineyard of choice varietals of foreign grapes, belonging to Jacob Schram. He also has a small cellar, and makes his own grapes into wine, which from its excellence, ranks among the best in the world."

Thus did contemporary historian, Campbell A. Menefee describe the Schramsburg Winery in his 1873 *Historical and Descriptive Sketchbook of Napa, Sonoma, Lake and Mendocino*. Jacob Schram had come to the Napa Valley in 1862, and by diligently saving his earnings as a barber, was able to purchase mountainside land and build a winery.

W.W. "Jack" Lyman remembers Schram as "energetic. He made a success of his life by his own energy and intelligence. He was a small man, with a round face who looked just like Santa Claus. He was very talkative, very much alive."

When Robert Louis Stevenson visited the Napa Valley in 1880, he went up to Schram's Winery and spend some time visiting, sampling and enjoying the Schrams' hospitality. He describes it all in his *Silverado Squatters*:

"Mr. Schram's on the other hand, is the oldest vineyard in the valley, eighteen years old I think; yet he began a penniless barber, and even after he had broken ground up here with his black malvoises, continued for long to tramp the valley with his razor. Now his place is the picture of prosperity: stuffed birds in the veranda, cellars far dug into the hillside, and resting on pillars like bandits cave: all trimness, varnish flowers, and sunshine, among the tangled wildwood. Stout, smiling Mrs. Schram, who had been in Europe and apparently all about the States for pleasure, entertained Fanny in the veranda, while I was tasting wine in the cellar. To Mr. Schram this was a solemn office; his serious gusto warmed my heart; prosperity had not yet wholly banished a certain neophite and girlish trepidation, and he followed every sip and read my face with proud anxiety. I tasted all. I tasted every variety and shade of Schramberger..."

Jacob Schram's wines were considered to be among the best of the time and many were served in better hotels and clubs both in this country and abroad. His success allowed him to build an impressive Victorian home upon whose veranda the Stevensons sat and sipped and talked. And, the home along with Schram's extensive dug-out caves, used to cellar his wine, are still serving their purposes for the current owner, Jack Davies and his Schramsburg Vineyards.

Jacob Schram's Winery, 1880

The beautifully preserved main building of Jacob Schram's Winery serves as the headquarters of Schramsburg Vineyards. Robert Louis Stevenson visited Schram here in 1880 and sipped wine on the veranda shown in this photo.

Captain Gustave Niebaum's Inglenook Winery, 1883   8

California's noted historian, Hubert Howe Bancroft writing in 1890 described Gustave Niebaum as "one of our leading business men and viniculturists." Apparently, judging from comments of others who knew him, Captain Niebaum would have heartily agreed with Bancroft.

A Finnish-Jew by birth, Niebaum began as a sailor in the service of the Russian American Company, in the far north. Before he was twenty-five, he had been promoted to the captaincy of a steamer. After the transfer of the Alaska territory to the United States, he tried his hand at seal hunting. He was so successful in his first season, that he raised the capital to purchase a partnership in what was to become the Alaska Commercial Company, and he also became the general manager of the firm.
In 1880, having entered into various branches of business, Niebaum purchased an 11,000 acre ranch and another 1,000 acre "estate" in the Napa Valley where he began to make wine. By 1884, he was turning out 110,000 gallons a vintage.

His vineyard purchase had included the name "Inglenook" or "cozy corner" and Niebaum set about to make his Inglenook Winery the best and most noted in California. Applying the same fervor to his winemaking that he had to his other ventures, Niebaum imported the finest cuttings and cooperage from Europe and carefully developed his winery.

Captain Niebaum realized his goal of excellence in winemaking when in 1889, Inglenook wines were awarded overall excellence awards at the Paris Exposition. And, they continued to do so until Niebaum's death in 1908.

Jack Lyman had known Captain Niebaum when he was about 10 years old, and his memories of the man are vivid:

"Niebaum was a very large man, broad-shouldered with a long, white beard down his chest. He had been a sea captain in the Alaska Commercial Company. He spoke Russian and had been in Russian service. In Alaska, he became a partner in the Alaska Commercial Company, and made a lot of money. He retired to the Napa Valley, bought land and built the wine cellar near his house.

Captain Niebaum was a massive-looking person. He spoke in a deep voice...He was cordial man and had a nice wife, quite pretty. Niebaum was well-respected, not a bit cantankerous. He was reserved. He regarded himself as an important person, and he was respected by everyone."

After Niebaum's death, his widow managed to continue in the tradition of exacting excellence until Prohibition forced the winery's closure. In 1933, Mrs. Niebaum reopened the winery with Carl Bundschu entrusted with the task of maintaining the Captain's high level of quality. Niebaum's grand-nephew later joined the winery and in the 1960's, surprised the wine world by selling Inglenook Vineyards to United Vintners. Thus ended a family-winemaking dynasty, and the way opened for corporate management of the valley's vineyards.

Captain Gustave Niebaum's Inglenook Winery, 1883, Napa Valley, California

Inglenook Winery is little changed from the time when Captain Gustave Niebaum first purchased his vineyard "Inglenook" or "cozy corner." The building has been in continuous use as a winery except for the period of Prohibition which forced its closure.

Home of Frederick Beringer, 1883 The Present Rhine House At Beringer Bros. Winery

9

WHEN THE BERINGER BROTHERS, Frederick and Jacob came to the Napa Valley in 1876, it was from a long background of winemaking. Their family had been involved with wine in Mainz, Germany and Frederick and Jacob had gone from there through the Medoc region in France to New York where they had a wine marketing operation. Yearning for vineyards and cellars of their own, they moved west to the Napa Valley. They were first employed by Charles Krug and Jacob continued to work there while Frederick moved down the road toward St. Helena and began to establish vineyards and construct a cellar.

The cellars at the Beringer Winery are almost as unique and interesting as is the Rhine House pictured on the drawing. Dug out by Chinese laborers using pick and shovels and small baskets to carry out the excess rubble, the "caves" are about 1000 feet of tunneling into the volcanic mountain behind the house.

The seventeen-room mansion, known as the Rhine House, was built by Frederick who seems, at least initially, to have had control of the winery operation. Jack Lyman remembers "Los Hermanos" (the Brothers):

"There were two brothers Beringer, Frederick (Fritz) and Jacob. Fritz had apparently inherited all of the family fortune, because he had the money. Fritz was a sharp man with side whiskers and a red face. He was always very talkative. His brother Jacob didn't have any money and he did the work. He was a very hard worker. Later Jacob Beringer bought out his older brother's share, so that Fritz's family disappeared and Jacob Beringer's remained.

"The Rhine House was built by Fritz and the story goes that it was modeled on the one they had had in Germany. They had come over in the 1870's. They were always entertaining.

"The Dutch elms must have gone in in front about the 1880's...(Lyman remembers them) about six feet tall."

For nearly 100 years the Beringer Brothers Winery remained in family hands, producing vintage every year since 1879. Even during Prohibition the winery produced wine for sacramental and medicinal purposes. An interesting note is that on December 6, 1933, the night of the repeal of the 18th Amendment ending Prohibition, the Beringers had six trucks at the winery loaded with cases of wine for delivery into the Bay Area. The Beringer Winery was one of the few that survived Prohibition intact.

In 1970, the winery and surrounding acreage was sold to Nestlé Company, Inc. by the Beringer family and since then it has been sold again.

The magnificence of Frederick and Jacob Beringer's Rhine House has been preserved though. And, visitors may enjoy the splendor while they sample premium Beringer wines in the downstairs area which serves as a tasting room and visitor facility.

Home of Frederick Beringer, 1883. The present Rhine House at Beringer Bros. Winery.
St. Helena, Napa Valley, California

© Otto Hesemeyer 1967

The Beringer mansion has seventeen rooms and retains the elegance and splendor its original builder intended. Today the former home serves as a visitor facility, offices and a tasting room for Beringer wines.

The Christian Brothers Wine and Champagne Cellars, 1888

NESTLED IN THE NAPA VALLEY between the Beringer Winery and the Charles Krug Stables is a beautiful old stone building: Greystone, or as it is more widely known, the Christian Brothers Winery. Built in the late 1880's by William B. Bourne, it was the largest stone winery in the world at the time. Unlike the Beringers or Jacob Schram who used Chinese labor for their stone work, Bourne employed emigrant Italian stonemasons, who had worked in the vineyards until their skill was realized.

Bourne built several houses near his stone winery, one of which his mother occupied. Bourne also had a home there although he never lived in it. His principal residence was San Francisco from which he could conduct his many businesses, among them mining, another sizeable vineyard in the Napa Valley and the company which supplied water to San Francisco. He did come up to the Napa Valley for months at a time; but, it was said that his heart was really in Ireland, and he spent much time abroad.

The Greystone winery itself was peculiar not only in its size but in its method of operation. It was custom winery, and many small neighboring vineyardists held subscriptions in it. During this period it was difficult financially, especially for the smaller

growers, to store their wines for aging. Large wine merchants would buy promising wine cheaply from growers who needed the capital to produce their next vintage; and store it in their warehouses until it was ready to be sold at a much higher price. Bourne and his partners at Greystone acted as their own bankers and advanced growers ten cents a gallon on all wines they took for storage. They took the must, or fresh-squeezed juice and made it into wine. Then when the wines matured and were sold, the growers too reaped the profit.

Unfortunately for Bourne and for the growers who would or could have used this Greystone "cooperative," phylloxera hit just as the winery got into operation and wine production fell drastically.

The winery then passed through several ownerships. At one time during the Depression of the 1930's, it was sold for an incredible $10,000, and this for a stone building with a floor space of just less than three acres.

William B. Bourne was quite a character himself. Owner of the celebrated Empire Mine in Grass Valley, California, he could afford to see his sometimes altruistic schemes through. Such was the case with his idea for a winery that could serve as a cooperative: where small growers could bring their young wines, get a cash advance that the banks refused to give on wine, and when the wine's promise was realized, sell it themselves and know the pride and profit of their fine wine. Thus Greystone was born. Jack Lyman remembers:

> "W.B.Bourne did things in a large way. He bought out a whole nursery of a man named Inman, who had a nursery below St. Helena. He bought the whole thing to plant in the grounds around the wine cellar, including the palm trees."

In 1950, the Greystone Winery was bought by the Christian Brothers. This order of Catholic teaching Brothers had been making wine in California, predominantly for sacramental purposes, since the 1880's. After suffering numerous setbacks, including bankruptcy after they had moved their Novitate and winery operations to the Napa Valley from Martinez in 1930, by producing fine quality wine and brandy, the Brothers made enough profit to gain clear title to their Novitiate and look beyond producing only sacramental and medicinal beverages. The Christian Brothers is now the largest winery in the Napa Valley, and the profits from the wines aged at Greystone as well as those produced at the other Brothers facilities, go to the support of their order and the many schools they have. We think that Mr. Bourne would approve of his winery's current use.

The Christian Brothers Wine and Champagne Cellars, 1888, St. Helena, Napa Valley, California

© Otto Hesemeyer 1967

When originally built as the Greystone Winery by William Bourne, this structure was the largest stone winery in the world. In 1950, the current occupants, the Christian Brothers took over the winery operation.

Freemark Abbey Cellars, 1895 (Formerly Lombardo Winery) 11

BEFORE ANTONIO FORNI began to erect his Lombarda Cellars in 1895, the property he had acquired had been used for wine-making, with a winemaker unique at that time for the Napa Valley—a woman. The ten acres upon which the winery is located was originally part of the "Carne Humana" land grant of Dr. E.T. Bale. It was inherited by his daughter Isadora and her husband, Louis Bruck. Ownership then passed through several hands until 1881, when John and Josephine Tychson acquired the land and its vineyards. They had hoped to become vintners and have their winery join the ranks of the best in California.

Unfortunately, a short time later, due to failing health, John Tychson took his own life. Josephine refused to follow the accepted pattern of that day and take her children to live with her family. She chose instead to build the winery that she and her husband had planned. It ran successfully for the following eight years until she turned it over to her foreman, Antonio Forni.

A newly-arrived Italian immigrant in the 1890's, Forni also broke with the patterns of the day. He first leased the Tychson winery and then began work on his own winery, "Lombarda Cellars," while his immigrant peers continued to labor in the fields of

other men. Completed in the early years of 1900, the winery building was constructed by Italian stonemasons using stone handcut from surrounding hills. Because of Forni's energy and perserverance, his winery continued in operation despite phylloxera and other obstacles until 1922.

Since 1922, there have been numerous owners, among them Albert M. Ahern, who taking ownership in 1938, first called it "Freemark Abbey." In 1965, a partnership of seven men acquired the winery, and although it is relatively new winery operation in the valley now, with its heritage of Josephine Tychson's determination and Antonio Forni's drive, the future seems to bode well for Freemark Abbey wines.

The solid stone walls of "Lombarda Winery" no longer house only a winery though. A resturant and several shops including a unique beeswax candle-factory now occupy the buildings. The original structure and its original purpose are still retained at Freemark Abbey, adding to the charm and character of the valley.

Freemark Abbey and the Christian Brothers Greystone Winery are excellent examples of Italian stonemasonry skill, while the cellars at both Beringer Winery and Schramsberg were created by Chinese stone masons. Within close geographical proximity of each other, these "survivors" afford the visitor the opportunity to observe and admire the stonework of these two immigrant people. It is fitting that these remarkable structures remain as monuments to their energy and skill.

Freemark Abbey Cellars, (formerly Lombarda Winery), 1895. Napa Valley, California

Today the Freemark Abbey Cellars houses a complex including a resturant and shops, but little has been architectually changed since Antonio Forni erected his Lombarda Cellars in 1895.

An Historic Winery and House, 1896 Present Heitz Cellars, Napa Valley, California

12

AS WAS MENTIONED PREVIOUSLY, there has been a trend in the Napa Valley in the second half of this century among young, educated winemakers to reclaim old vineyards and produce exceptional but relatively small vinages using new, more scientific methods. Joseph Heitz is an excellent example of this new genre of winemakers.

Heitz, who is not related to the old Heitz family in the Calistoga area, had come to the Napa Valley in 1951. In 1961, he bought eight acres of vineyard planted in Grignolino grapes and a highway-side tasting room from Leon Brendel. Joseph Heitz was not a newcomer to winemaking, having worked at several wineries, including Beaulieu and having taught enology and viticulture at Fresno State College. Later, in 1964, Heitz purchased another winery and vineyard at the end of Taplin Road on the eastern side of the valley. The Spring Valley Ranch had at one time been in vineyard but a previous owner had pulled out the old vines and it was in pasture when Heitz acquired it. The winery which is pictured on the drawing had been built by A. Rossi in the late 1890's, although he had produced wine earlier. In fact, Rossi's 1880 vintage was composed of 10,000 gallons of wine.

As late as Prohibition, the property was functioning as a vineyard and winery. In fact, during Prohibition, when a San Francisco restauranteer owned it, they developed an interesting method of concealing their product, which seems to have been known to several other valley winemakers as well. When it was learned that Federal agents might make a raid, the barrels were drained of their wine into small casks, and crates were stacked around them hiding the forbidden product. The vineyard acreage actually increased at the ranch by 50% during Prohibition. It seems that here, as in much of the rest of the industry, no one's heart was truly in Prohibition.

After the Heitz' took over, they began planting the vineyards again in 1966-67. Presently the Joseph Heitz Winery is producing some of the finest and most outstanding wines in the valley, and indeed in the world. And it is at the same time, preserving the charm of an old winery.

What men and women like Joseph Heitz have achieved is a fulfillment of Robert Louis Stevenson's prophecy made in 1880:

"Wine in California is still in the experimental stage...The beginning of vine-planting is like the beginning of mining for the precious metals: the wine grower also "prospects": One corner of land after another is tried with one kind of grape after another. This is a failure; that is better; a third best. So bit by bit, they grope about for their Clos Vouget and Lafite. Those lodes and pockets of earth, more precious than the precious ores, that yield the inimitable fragrance and soft fire; whose virtuous Bonanzas, where the soil has sublimated under sun and stars to something finer, and the wine is bottled poetry: these still lie undiscovered; chaparral conceals, thicket embowers them...But there they bid their hour, awaiting their Columbus; and nature nurses and prepares them. The smack of California earth shall linger on the palate of your grandson."

The Napa Valley's hour would truly seem to be now. And, with luck, and the winemaker's skill, our grandchildren will too enjoy the fruit of the Napa Valley vineyardists' labors.

An Historical Winery and Home, 1896. Present Heitz Wine Cellars, Napa Valley, California.

This close-up view of the Heitz Wine Cellars shows the detail of the stone work so often utilized in many of the Napa Valley's surviving structures.

Original Foundry, 1884 St. Helena, Napa Valley, California

13

"The Hatchery (originally the Foundry) is one of several stone commercial warehouse buildings constructed along Railroad Avenue (St. Helena) in the 1880's, convenient to the Southern Pacific Depot for loading and unloading. The buildings comprise a unique 19th century warehouse district whose buildings have been converted to a variety of 20th century commerical uses. The Hatchery, a two story, trapezoidal shaped building of coursed native fieldstone, has a hipped gable roof. Arches of the doorways and windows are semi-circular with radiating stones. The exterior of the Hatchery is unaltered though the interior has been modified."

THUS READS THE 1978 description of the Original Foundry (or as it was then known, the Hatchery) in the Napa County Historical Resources Survey registration.

In the year 1884, the firm of Taylor, Duckworth and company had built the stone building pictured in this drawing and in it established their foundry business. A page one advertisement in the *St. Helena Star* of that year stated:

Taylor, Duckworth & Co., Proprietors

St. Helena Foundry, Planing Mill, Box Factory, Barley Crusher

This firm are now making a specialty of wine presses, and will build any kind of screw and toggle or hydraulic press. All kinds of castings, turning, planing and sawing in lumber. Grape boxes a speciality.

Mr. Duckworth tried unsuccessfully to operate the St. Helena Electric Light and Power Company in the building after he converted it from a foundry just before 1890. In 1900, it was owned for a few months by an attorney, Theodore Bell, who then sold it to E.H. Raymond. Mr. Raymond it seems was forced by labor unrest in San Francisco to move his leather glove manufacturing business. And, he established his Factory #2 in the Foundry building. For five years from 1906 to 1911, it was owned by the Napa Investment Company who then sold it back to Raymond. Despite the changes in ownership, it was operated as a glove factory until the end of World War I.

From 1926 to 1958, the building was owned by Dan Gardner of St. Helena. It was probably used only for storage during this time, although by one account, Gardner used it as a hatchery. Mr. Albert Hawke of Calistoga purchased it in 1958 and operated it as a hatchery, thus the name that it is commonly known by. After Mr. Hawke's death, the Vailima Foundation purchased it and established a Robert Louis Stevenson museum in it. The museum with its unmatched collection of Stevenson manuscripts and memorabilia occupied the building, along with a resturant until 1979, when the museum moved into the new St. Helena library. The building's current (1980) owners, Mr. and Mrs. Mark Bauer are very interested in their building's history and it seems that the Old Foundry/ Glove Factory/ Hatchery will remain a monument of the valley's earlier industries for some time to come.

Original Foundry, 1884, St. Helena, Napa Valley, California

Even today, much of St. Helena's architecture reflects an earlier era as suggested in the photo. The building shown has been used for many puposes, but the exterior has been unaltered since its original erection.

Old Pope Street Bridge, Silverado Trail St. Helena, 1890, Napa Valley, California

14

AS THE ORIGINAL FOUNDRY stands a monument to the industry in the Napa Valley in the 19th century, the Pope Street Bridge stands a monument to the ingenuity and aesthetic appreciation of that time. At the turn of the century, Napa County was known as the "County of the Stone Bridges." Between sixty and seventy bridges were built across the Napa River and its tributaries. The Putah Creek Bridge, at the time called the "Queen of Stone Bridges," was said to be the largest stone bridge west of the Rocky Mountains. It is now under Lake Berryessa, but the Pope Street Bridge still stands and still accomodates traffic while reminding us of another era of highway construction.

A plaque on the bridge, which is located at the junction of Pope Street and the Silverado Trail near St. Helena, reads:

Erected 1894. Town Trustees: H.M. Pond, H.L. Chiles, C.H. Anderson, R.H. Pithie, Contractor.

The bridge itself cost $13,000 when it was built and was the only bridge in the county which was a joint city/county venture. R.H. Pithie, the contractor, was a Scottish stonemason. He seems to have been well-respected as a builder and is thought to have had a great deal to do with Napa County becoming noted for its bridges.

Almost all of the workmen on the Pope Street Bridge were Italian stonemasons and the somewhat unique design they used here may in part explain why so many of the valley's stone bridges are still in use. The piers were built with their supports leaning outward at the bottom to repel water-driven logs and other debris which the Napa River took downstream as it flooded.

The Pope Street Bridge connected St. Helena with the Silverado Trail via Pope Street. The Trail had started out as just that, an Indian trail. It has since served as a major arterial for the Napa Valley. This stone bridge, as well as Pope Creek and Pope Valley, adjacent to the Napa Valley, all owe their nomenclature to William Pope. As an early pioneer of the area, Pope held the grant of land known as the Locoallomi Rancho. It had been transmitted to him as a land grant from acting governor Manuel Jimeño in September, 1841. The grant was comprised of two leagues (8823 acres) in what is today Pope Valley.

Having originally lived in the East, William Pope arrived in this area, by way of New Mexico where he had taken a native wife. A somewhat romantic character, Pope had at one time been a beaver trapper. However, that career was ended in his arrest in San Diego for entering Mexico without proper papers. Fortunately for our story, this trapper moved on north and became a prominent rancher in the Napa County area and left us his eternal mark.

Though the Pope Street Bridge was not particularly unique in its time, it has by its survival become unique in preserving the usefulness and beauty of an earlier highway system.

Old Pope Street Bridge, Silverado Trail, St. Helena, 1890, Napa Valley, California

This recent photo shows one of the original 60 bridges which once crossed the Napa River and its tributaries. Known as the "County of Stone Bridges," the Pope Street Bridge still graces Napa County with its simple elegance.

The Original Stone Bridge Saloon, And ! St. Helena, California, 1902

15

"On a warm Sunday afternoon, June 20, 1920, the popular Stone Bridge House was destroyed by fire. The bar stopped pouring, the girls ceased working, the patrons hurriedly left and St. Helena's notorious joy house and palace of pleasure was reduced to ashes. All that was left was man's pleasant memories of gay hours and lively nights well spent."

THE ABOVE obituary for the St. Helena institution known as the Stone Bridge Saloon appeared in the *St. Helena Star*. Although the owner, Madame Krueger reopened soon at a nearby house she also owned, the Original Stone Bridge Saloon remains only in this drawing and in men's memories. Built in the 1880's, the saloon was on the bluff facing Stone Bridge, across the river from the churches. It was well-known, if not frequented, by young men of the valley for more than a half-century. It was very plainly, a bar and house of prostitution

It would belabor the point to go into more detail about the saloon's business enterprises or its clients. Suffice it to say that the Napa Valley had a bit of most kinds of commerce operating within it at one time or another.

Although no monument remains to mark the Original Stone Bridge House, it is well-memoralized in the twinkle of the eye of those who remember it and its place in Napa Valley history.

The Original Stone Bridge Saloon, and! St. Helena, California, 1902

Since 1920, nothing has remained of the Stone Bridge Saloon except fond tales and memories. However, through those tales it is still a, "Survivor of the Past," in the Napa Valley.